dance on the
dusty earth

dance on the
dusty earth

by christine price

CHARLES SCRIBNER'S SONS

NEW YORK

Illustration on page 1:
POLYNESIAN DANCER Cook Islands
Pages 2-3:
AFRICAN DANCER Sierra Leone
Below: AFRICAN DANCER Zaire
Opposite: YOUNG THAI DANCER
Playing the part of the monkey, Hanuman

This book is for Charles Moore

Copyright © 1979 Christine Price

Library of Congress Cataloging in Publication Data
Price, Christine, 1928-
    Dance on the dusty earth.
    SUMMARY: Examines the folk dances of many cultures
which have been handed down from one generation to the
next.
    1. Folk dancing—Juvenile literature   [1. Folk
dancing]   I. Title.
GV1743.P74   793.3'1   78-25714
ISBN 0-684-16088-9

contents

THE OTHER WORLD OF DANCE   6

LEAP TO THE SKY   18

HANDS THAT TELL STORIES   25

DANCES OF WAR   34

MAGIC CIRCLES   45

BEND TO THE EARTH   56

DANCE MAP   62

the other world of dance

TWO lines of dancers with sprays of green leaves in their hands come trotting down the dusty plaza. Men in white kilts, woven sashes, and waistbands of jingling bells alternate with women in black dresses, bright silk capes, and white leggings. The singers have begun their chant. The drummer is sounding a steady beat, its rhythm echoed by the bells and rattles of the dancers.

Halfway down the plaza, the two lines turn to face each other in front of a little shrine like an open tent. The entrance is decorated with freshly cut saplings and tree branches, bright green with new spring leaves. Inside, on the altar at the back, stands a figure of Saint Anthony, whose feast-day is today. The Indians of the pueblo celebrate the feast with dances.

The women's feet, barely lifted with each step, seem to caress the earth. The green twigs in their hands wave in time to the rhythm. While the women and girls hold their places in the lines, the men and boys surge forward to meet in the center, and then retreat, shaking their rattles.

The rhythm of drum and song controls the dancers, even the smallest ones bobbing up and down at the ends of the lines. They need no audience. They never glance at the silent watchers scattered along the edges of the plaza. The dancers are held spellbound by the patterns of the dance.

Today they honor the saint whose small image stands on the altar, but their dance is much older than the coming of Christian saints to the Indian pueblo. The people dance as their ancestors did, long before the white men appeared in their land. The movement of their bodies is a ceremony, and the dusty plaza between the earth-brown adobe houses is a holy place, filled with the ancient magic of dance.

That magic is known to people the world over. In almost every land, since the first men walked the earth, people have had the urge to dance.

8

Birds and beasts and insects were the first dancers, using a language of movement more vivid than words. Perhaps, for the first human beings, this language of the whole body came before speech. Perhaps they danced their joy and their sorrow, the triumph of a successful hunt or the pain and fear they felt when a hunter was killed.

In the dance, the common movements of everyday life—walking, running, leaping, and stretching—were made into new patterns, given new meaning and a new mysterious power. Movements became the raw materials of art. Some say that dance is the oldest of all the arts. The maker of a dance needs no tools. What he has to say is expressed by the strong bodies of the dancers, and the work of art is a living, moving thing.

The love of dancing is as natural as the love of life, for the movement, rhythm, and pattern that make up the language of dance are the signs of life itself. To be alive is to move in rhythm. Stillness comes only with death. Even when we are asleep, we move in rhythm. The lungs breathe in and out. The steady drumbeat of the heart sends the blood dancing through the arteries and veins.

Beyond the rhythms of our bodies are the vast rhythms of the earth and sky. The whole universe moves in rhythm. The rhythmic patterns of day and night, summer and winter govern the lives of all living things. All creatures, from earthworms to eagles and from blades of grass to giant redwood trees, are performers in one great dance.

Stone Age hunters were as much a part of the natural world as animals and plants. Even when people learned to farm the land and rear domestic animals, they were still obedient to the rhythms of nature. Their dances were echoes of those rhythms.

The circle of the seasons was marked by dance. In cold northern lands, dancers greeted the turn of the year, when the sun had conquered the darkness of winter and the shortened days began to grow long again. North and south, east and west, farmers danced

Here and on page 9:
ABORIGINAL DANCERS
WITH BODY PAINT
Australia

DANCING PRIEST
Mayan clay figure
Mexico, 700-1000 A.D.

at planting time and harvest. There were special dances too for the important happenings in people's personal lives—for births and deaths and weddings, and for the coming-of-age of young boys and girls.

Both hunters and farmers danced in imitation of animals. Some believed they had animal ancestors, and for many peoples, animals were gods.

Many of the earliest dances must have been linked with the belief in gods and spirits, the unseen rulers of earth and sky. Body movement could be a form of prayer, to call down blessings and to win the help of gods. Farmers would dance to bring rain to thirsty fields, just as hunters danced for good luck in hunting, and warriors for courage in battle. Medicine men danced to cure people of sickness, and when a prayer was granted, dance was a way of giving thanks.

The Bible tells how the Children of Israel, freed at last from slavery in Egypt, praised God with dancing and music. Even David, King of Israel, was not ashamed to dance before the Ark of the Lord.

11

Opposite:
GREEK DANCER
Clay figure, 2nd cent. B.C.
EGYPTIAN DANCERS
Tomb painting, 2500 B.C.

DANCING SHIVA
Indian bronze sculpture

In India, the worshippers of the god Shiva called him Lord of the Dance, for his wonderful performance at the creation of the world had brought order to the universe. Temple dancers, dedicated to the service of the gods, practiced their sacred art in the temples of India.

12

The ancient temples of Egypt, Greece, and Rome were also the scene of marvelous festivals of dance; and when the first Christian missionaries began to spread the faith, nearly two thousand years ago, dancing became a part of worship in Christian churches.

During the Middle Ages, often called the Age of Faith, dances in church were banned in most parts of Europe as pagan and sinful things. But no one could stop people dancing for pleasure on village greens or in the streets of cities. There were also splendid spectacles of dance and pantomime in the palaces of kings. Rulers and noblemen had been patrons of the dance since the time of the pharaohs in ancient Egypt, and some of the finest dancing was presented as palace entertainment. In Italy, France, and England in the sixteenth century these royal displays gave birth to the art of ballet.

**EARLY BALLET
DANCERS**
Left to right: 18th,
16th, and 17th centuries

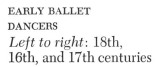

Ballet was born at an exciting time. Men of Europe were ranging far over the world and bringing back glittering treasures and strange tales from Asia and the newly found Americas. The stage was set for a new form of art that combined dancing with exotic costumes and scenery and dramatic stories.

Courtiers at the royal palaces were the first ballet dancers, moving in stately measures before audiences of invited guests. But the new art was too thrilling to be restricted to the court. By the beginning of the eighteenth century the dancers were trained professionals, and ballets were performed in public theaters for all to see. People sat spellbound as the dancers soared like birds across the stage. Ballet enchanted its audiences with a new kind of magic, carrying them away to a land of dreams. It was an escape from life, not an echo of life's rhythms. Dance, presented in the theater, had lost touch with the earth. The old magic had passed away.

Today, we tend to think of dance as entertainment, whether it is social dancing to the music of popular songs, or an evening of ballet. Dance performances in theaters and concert halls can offer us thrills and laughter, tragedy, mystery, and the pure delight of rhythmic movement and pattern. Classical ballet is only one of many forms of dance. In the brilliant world of the dancer and choreographer there is always something new to be discovered.

Yet what seems so new may have grown from ancient roots. Some choreographers, creating new dances, are trying to bring back the old magic of dance. They look for ideas in a world that lies far beyond the theaters and the noise of city streets. There, the stage is the dusty ground, and the rhythms of earth and sky are strongly felt in the lives of the people and in their dancing.

MOVEMENTS FROM
AFRICAN AND
HAITIAN DANCE

The Pueblo Indians, honoring the saint in the leafy shrine, belong to that other world of dance. With them are American Indians of many tribes; and beyond the Americas there are peoples in Asia, Africa, and the islands of the South Pacific for whom the dance has never lost its ancient magic.

Time has not stood still for these people. Their lifeways and their reasons for dancing have changed with the passing years. But dances that are important to them have been handed down from one generation to the next. Young children, like the small Indians in the pueblo plaza, are taught the dances that their ancestors knew.

Exploring that other world of dance may take us to the dim beginnings of the dancer's art. Though no one can tell exactly what the earliest dances were like, there are a few clues to follow. Body movements and dance patterns have been recorded in paintings, rock carvings, and sculptures by artists of long ago. We can see how people leaped and skipped and moved in circles, how warriors danced with sword and shield, and hunters mimicked animals.

These same movements and patterns can come alive for us today in the other world of dance. We must search for the dancers on the dusty earth. Under the blazing sun or in the dark of midnight they can still show us, in their many ways, the ancient magic of the dance.

DANCERS IN CLAY SCULPTURE
Opposite page: Greece, 6th cent. B.C.
Above: Mexico, 300 A.D.

leap to the sky

THE women and girls are dancing in Lokorua's homestead. This is a great day for Lokorua and his people. Two of the young men are going through the Sapana ceremony. By the day's end they will wear on their heads a close-fitting cap of hardened mud, painted blue and trimmed with white ostrich feathers. For the Pokot people of East Africa, this is the sign of a grown man and a warrior.

Lokorua is a leader among the Pokot, a rich man with several wives and many children. His homestead is a cluster of small domed huts, no more than shelters for sleeping. His wealth is in his magnificent herd of goats, camels, and beautiful long-horned cattle. For the sake of the animals, he and his family never stay long in one place. When the herd needs fresh grazing grounds, the people must move on.

Early this morning, before the animals had been taken out to feed, a fine goat was chosen for sacrifice and killed with a single spear-blow. This marked the beginning of the Sapana.

Now it is noon. The first coating of mud has been carefully molded on the heads of the two young men and must be left to dry before the ceremony goes on. The men and boys are resting in the noonday heat. The women and girls have started to celebrate with song and dance.

The sound of their voices comes from the bare open space inside the circle of huts. There, under the hot sun, the women are singing and clapping while a group of girls leap into the air together, hand in hand. The girls come down with a thud and a clash of leg-rattles, then leap again and again in time with the song.

Then the dance pattern changes. The women form a long chain, holding onto each other's waists. With small shuffling steps they follow the leader in a dance they call the Snake, until suddenly the shouts of men cut through the women's songs.

Men and boys, armed with spears, appear between the huts. Stamping and shouting, they pour into the dancing place, and the women scatter before them.

19

The men crouch down in a circle, and an old one begins to sing. He sings of war and the work of the warrior, and the others respond with mellow, deep-toned humming. Then the men spring up to perform a stamping circle dance, a snake dance, and a mime of battle. Finally, to the sound of singing from all the people, small groups of men begin to leap.

Their long, lean legs are like steel springs. The men seem to hang in the air, coming down flat-footed on the bare earth, then springing up still higher with the quickening rhythm of the songs. The dust rises in clouds. Sweat streams from the dark skins of the dancers. The women join in the dance with the men,

drawn into the circle of leaping figures. The rhythm grows faster and faster. The dancers are packed together more closely, surging through the haze of dust, and leaping, tireless, to the great pale sky.

The leaping dance of the Pokot is the age-old dance of cattle herders, nomadic folk who wander far and scorn to settle down. For Lokorua and his people, the earth is for cattle, not for crops. Cattle are their wealth, their life, and their joy. The blood and milk of cattle are the warriors' food, and the names of the fighting men are the names of oxen.

Every warrior has an ox whose name he has taken as his own. He loves his name-ox, trains its horns to grow in beautiful shapes, and sings songs in its praise. The ox-songs that he makes are the music of the dance, and even the way of dancing seems molded by life with the cattle.

Following their herds over the wide land, the people must walk for miles and never tire. So their dance is a dance of the legs. As the strong legs of the Pokot dancers send them higher and higher, reaching for the sky, their bodies are straight as spearshafts and their arms are held close to their sides.

22

Yet arms and hands can often speak more clearly than legs in the language of the dance. Far across the world from Lokorua's country are people for whom the arms are all-important in dancing. Hands can tell stories, and legs may have so little part to play that some of the finest dances are performed while sitting down.

POLYNESIAN
STORYTELLING DANCE
Cook Islands

MUDRA MEANING
DEER OR COW

INDIAN DANCER AS
SHIVA, LORD OF THE DANCE
Left: MOVEMENT FROM
INDIAN TEMPLE DANCE

24

hands that tell stories

I N India, the hands of the dancer are trained in a language of their own. Whole stories can be told by the positions of the hands, called *mudras*. They can represent a deer, a bird, or a budding lotus flower. The hands can also express feelings of love and longing, sorrow, anger, or defiance.

The language of *mudras* was first described by a wise man of India named Bharata, about two thousand years ago. He was said to have learned the secrets of dance from the gods themselves, and the book he wrote, *The Science of Dancing*, has been followed ever since by performers of Indian dance.

MUDRAS
Left to right:
World; bird;
budding lotus;
love; war.

The techniques of Indian dancing described in Bharata's book were carried eastward to other lands of Asia, where Indians traveled to trade. Court dancers, performing in the royal palaces of Burma and Cambodia, Thailand and Indonesia, learned movements in the Indian style. Their arms and hands were trained to be miraculously supple and expressive, but the complicated language of the *mudras* was simplified. However much the dancers learned from India, each country gave its own character to the dance.

26

On the tiny island of Bali, off the eastern tip of Java, the Hindu faith and the Indian traditions of temple dancing became firmly rooted. Bali today is still a land of dance. Along with performances of old dances, there are exciting new ones. In the Kebyar, created in recent times by one of Bali's greatest dancers, the young performer is seated with his legs folded under him. He must dance only with his body, his head, and his expressive hands and arms.

27

Sitting dances can also be seen among the island peoples of the South Pacific, far beyond the shores of Asia. On the many small islands of Micronesia, north of New Guinea, the people were famous in the past as bold navigators. Their lives centered around the swift canoes in which they made long sea voyages. Sitting dances were often performed in the narrow space of the canoe-house, close to the beach, or even aboard the canoe itself.

28

The Polynesians were equally renowned as seafarers. They made their homes on hundreds of islands, from New Zealand in the south to Hawaii in the north; and wherever they settled they brought with them their love of dancing. In their "action songs," they tell epic tales of the ancient Polynesian explorers, who set out across the unknown ocean to find new lands. As the story is chanted by the singers, men may mimic the action of paddling a canoe, while the arms of the seated women ripple like waves of the sea.

POLYNESIAN
ACTION SONG
Maori people,
New Zealand

For the people of Western Samoa, in the heart of Polynesia, no celebration is complete without dance. They call a celebration a *fia-fia*, and when one is planned to honor guests in a village, the best dancers spend many hours in rehearsal.

The *fia-fia* takes place in the big round meeting house in the middle of the village. It is a warm starry night, and the house has no walls to shut out the soft breeze. The lofty domed roof is supported by a ring of thick wooden posts and a single great pillar in the center, where a space is left clear for dancing. The people sit on mats on the floor, the guests on the left of the entrance, and a big crowd of villagers on the right. Musicians on the villagers' side are ready to make music with guitars and with a rolled-up mat that serves as a drum. An oil lamp hanging from the central pillar casts a glow over the dancing floor and the sea of expectant faces.

At last the performers enter—a long procession of women, young and old. Their three leaders take places of honor on the mats just inside the entrance. The eldest makes a solemn speech, and then, with a whoop and a burst of music, the dancing begins.

A woman comes reeling and stumbling onto the dancing floor. She is the clown who will make fun of the other dancers. The first group of women follows her, with small steps and undulating gestures of their arms; and one after another, fresh groups rise up to dance. Some enter with the clicking rhythm of coconut shells like castanets, others with the sharp slapping of hands on knees and thighs. Even the largest, stoutest women move with an easy grace in their loose cotton gowns or gay wraparound *lavalavas* and garlands of flowers. A long line of women sways in unison, arms rippling, hands pointing. Then they begin to reach out and beckon to the audience. Young men leap to their feet and join the dance. Squatting down low, their arms spread wide, the men circle around the dancing women, who never allow themselves to be touched.

More and more people, young and old, invade the dancing floor. The formality of the women's dances dissolves into a happy mass of swaying figures. The meeting house is filled with a swirl of color, the movement of graceful limbs shining with coconut oil, the scent of flowers, and the sweep of long dark hair.

Tonight the women have held the stage. On another night the young men will have a chance to display their most spectacular dance. For this, the *fia-fia* should be held outdoors, under the stars.

The dancing place is a grassy clearing surrounded by coconut palms. The audience, sitting on the ground, sees a flare of yellow flame in the darkness, and a young dancer comes bounding into the open. He is naked except for a short loincloth and a wreath of flowers, and in his hands are two bush-knives, each with a flaming torch at the tip of the blade and the butt of the handle.

While the drumsticks batter on the matting drum, the dancer juggles with the torches, tosses them up and catches them, and whirls them like fiery wheels. He opens his mouth and holds the flames against his tongue. He passes the torches behind his back, throws himself onto the grass, and balances them on the soles of his feet.

Then a second fire dancer leaps out of the shadows. They whirl their torches in unison, and while the watchers shrink back and hold their breath, the flaming knives fly through the air, back and forth between the dancers.

The Samoan fire dance gives us a vision of the heroes of long ago, when warriors danced with their weapons before they went to war. Dances of war were more than mere mimes of battle or celebrations of victory after the fighting was over.

In ancient Greece, it was said that only good dancers made good warriors. The body trained for dance was trained for battle. In his dancing the warrior lost all fear and proved his strength and skill.

WARRIOR'S DANCE
From an ancient Greek relief

dances of war

THE boom of drums, the squeal of woodwinds, and the flash of curved blades in the sun—all the bravado of the swordsman is in the sword dance of the men of Hunza, high in the Himalayas.

Hunza is a land of heroes, famous as warriors, dancers, musicians, and players of polo. The land and its people seem larger than life. Whether or not the people live to be over a hundred, as some have said, old men of Hunza can dance as nimbly as boys. All the best dancers have their own tunes, as the best polo-players do, for even polo games are played to music.

The courtyard that is the scene of the sword danc-ing is like a shelf carved out of the mountainside. The row of thundering drummers is seated along the outer edge, where the ground drops off to the valley far below. Their leader is the player of the *shenai*, an oboelike instrument with a piercing, reedy tone. He is playing the special music for the best-known sword dancer, and a cheer goes up from the crowd of people in the courtyard as the dancer steps out with a bright sword in each hand.

He faces the musicians and begins to dance with the swords over his shoulders, his back straight as a gun barrel and his feet making small, neat steps. Sud-denly the swords flash upwards, and with a twist of his wrists, the blades are horizontal, the points pressed to his temples. Then the swords are whipped under his arms and held close against his body.

Finally, as the drums beat louder with rattle and boom, and the voice of the *shenai* rises to a scream, the dancer draws near to the musicians and whirls the swords in glittering circles. The crowd roars until even the thunder of the drums is smothered. Only the squeal of the *shenai* pierces through the din.

The *shenai* player sways to and fro, with one hand on his instrument and the other reaching out to the dancer. Through all the effort of making music, his face is alight with joy. Musician and dancer are caught up together in the magic of the dance.

WAR DANCE
Iban people,
Sarawak

The chosen weapon of the men of Hunza is the sword. For Iban warriors in the tropical forests of Sarawak, in northern Borneo, it is the *parang*, a long heavy knife. The Ibans were headhunters in the past, and though they live in peace now, in their long-houses beside the forest rivers, they have not forgotten their dances of war.

Night is the time for dancing, when warm darkness blankets the forest. In the Iban longhouse, perched high on stilts above the river beach, the day's work is done. Men, women, and children are ready to enjoy themselves.

The house is the home of a whole community, and most of the people are sitting on the floor of the passageway in front of the rooms where the different families live.

37

Halfway down the passage, a few lamps hang from the rafters, making an island of light outside the headman's door. Here the musicians are seated with a drum, a set of small metal gongs, and two big hanging gongs that gleam gold in the lamplight. As they start to play, their rippling music fills the house.

One of the men has been pulled from his seat on the floor and persuaded to dance. There is joking and laughter while he straps a *parang* to his waist and takes a few hesitant steps in the lamplit dancing space. Then the magic of the dance seems to enter into him. His smile fades, and his face has a look of dreaming. He rises on his toes and begins his dance with beautiful spiral movements of arms and body, followed by deep knee-bends and turns.

Then he draws the *parang* from its patterned sheath and picks up a wooden shield. The dance becomes a mime of battle. He circles, crouching low; he leaps with a hoarse shout; he bends backward, almost to the floor, with the shield covering his body. The muscles swell under his smooth brown skin, which is tattooed on body, arms, and throat with a rich tapestry of dark blue designs. He moves with a catlike grace, the *parang* shining dully in his hand. This is the dance of a man of the forest, a lone warrior stalking his enemy in the deep shade of the trees. . . .

Solo dances of war, like this one, display the skill and courage of the individual warrior. In the great group dances, whole armies of men were once fired with the spirit of battle.

IBAN WAR DANCE
Each dancer makes
his own variations

Scores of leaping, charging warriors would join in the *haka*, the terrifying war dance of the Maori people of New Zealand. Though warfare is no longer a way of life for the Maori, the *haka* is still danced with all the zest and fury of the days of old.

Many other island peoples of the South Pacific remember the war dances of the past and perform them with pride. These dances range from the dramatic *meke* of the men of Fiji with their clubs or spears to a menacing war dance of the Solomon Islands, performed without music or song. The only sound is the *step-STAMP! step-STAMP!* of bare feet on the earth, as the warriors advance, their dark skins streaked with white paint, their arms outstretched before them, bearing axe and shield.

WAR DANCE
Maori people,
New Zealand

40

Farther north in the Pacific, on the islands of Micronesia, there are warlike stick dances that can be as exciting and challenging as any dance with weapons.

On the island of Yap, the stick dance is performed by men and girls together. They arrange themselves in two lines facing each other. One of the men lets out a high-pitched whoop, and with answering shouts the dancers cross sticks—*crack! crack!*—first with their partners opposite, and then with those beside them. The swift rhythm of the beating sticks is the rhythm of the dance.

CLUB DANCE Fiji

41

As the pace quickens, the two lines break into shifting groups of fours. Single dancers run from group to group, diving into battle yet never breaking the rhythm of the beating sticks. The dancers work in short bursts with rests between. Each bout of dancing, beginning at a moderate pace, gets faster and faster and mounts to a climax with a furious *whack-whack-whack!* of the sticks.

Another dance of war, well-loved in Yap, is the marching dance. The performers are young girls, who carry no weapons. Their cheeks are painted red, and they wear bead necklaces, flowery garlands, and full dancing skirts that swing about their hips. The group is led by a tall woman, who marches beside them and sings, loud and clear, the verses of the dancing song.

At her shouted order, the girls line up facing the audience and begin to mark time like soldiers. They stamp their feet and swing their arms vigorously back and forth, with an extraordinary look of boredom on their painted faces. Then the leader starts a new verse of the song, and the girls swirl around in a joyous rhythm. They crouch down, slap arms and thighs, and rise up with a supple shaking of their hips. The orders to march come again, like a chorus between the verses, and at once the girls begin their monotonous stamping.

The audience dissolves into gales of laughter. The dance is a mockery of war, not war as the island people knew it in the past, but the stiff military drill of the white men. In this new dance, composed after the white men had come to dominate the islands, the ancient language of movement speaks more clearly than words, as in the oldest dances of all.

CIRCLE DANCES
Above: American Indian
From a painting by John White, 1585
Center: New Guinea
Far right: Ancient Mexico

magic circles

THE oldest form of dance pattern is the circle. All living creatures, human and animal, tend to move in curves, and everywhere in the world people dance in circles. The circle was not only the natural shape for the first dances, but also for many of the things that people made, like round huts for shelter, round baskets, and round pots of clay.

In dance, the circle may be large and open, or small and tightly closed, with the dancers holding hands or linking arms. But large or small, the circle is always the same, a mysterious perfect form, without beginning or end.

A simple circle dance is performed by Lambadi women of South India, tall, handsome, and gypsylike in their swinging skirts, bright headshawls, and silver jewelry. Among the Lambadi people, only the women are dancers, and the music for this dance is their own singing. When the melody falls in pitch, they all bend down to the center of the circle with swaying arms and jingling ankle bells. Then as the song rises high, the dancers rise with it and lift their arms above their heads. This is a dance of joy, and the same song-phrase and movements are repeated over and over.

WOMEN'S CIRCLE DANCE
Lambadi people, India
Left: CLAY FIGURE
Ancient Egypt, 4000 B.C.

When instruments make music for a circle dance, the musicians usually stand in the center with the dancers revolving around them. But sometimes the players themselves are the dancers. In a celebration dance of the Bontoc people, who live high in the mountains of northern Luzon in the Philippines, the men make their own music with gongs.

In West Africa, the Senufo people of the Ivory Coast have an exciting circle dance, performed at night around a blazing fire. Here, the drummers and players of xylophones, with their instruments hung from their shoulders, move in a tireless circle around the dancers. Young men, showing off their swift foot-work, form the innermost circle, with the women moving more sedately around them. The supple bodies of the dancers and the tall striding figures of the musicians in their fantastic feathered hats are silhouetted against the yellow flames.

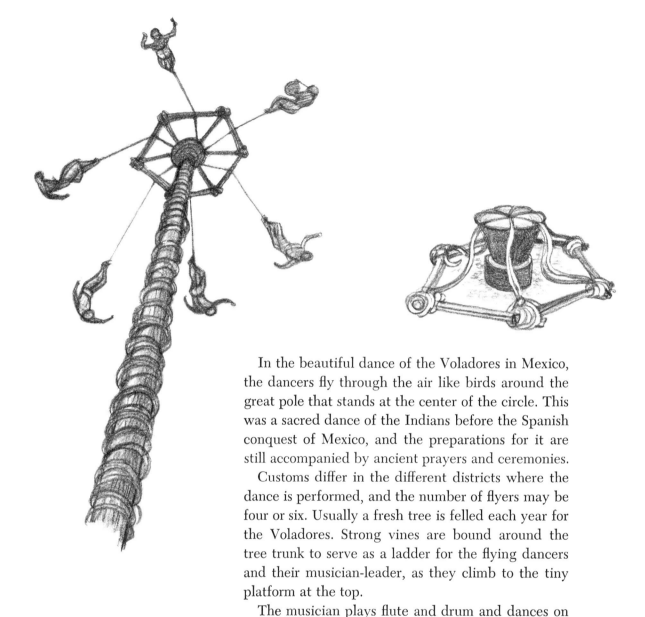

In the beautiful dance of the Voladores in Mexico, the dancers fly through the air like birds around the great pole that stands at the center of the circle. This was a sacred dance of the Indians before the Spanish conquest of Mexico, and the preparations for it are still accompanied by ancient prayers and ceremonies.

Customs differ in the different districts where the dance is performed, and the number of flyers may be four or six. Usually a fresh tree is felled each year for the Voladores. Strong vines are bound around the tree trunk to serve as a ladder for the flying dancers and their musician-leader, as they climb to the tiny platform at the top.

The musician plays flute and drum and dances on the dizzy height of the platform. Then the flyers, each with a rope around his body, launch themselves into space. They circle the pole thirteen times while the ropes unwind and gradually let them down to earth. The musician plays on, alone in the sky, until the flyers have landed. He is still playing when he slides headfirst down two ropes held taut by the men below.

VOLADORES
BEGINNING
THEIR DESCENT
Pahuatlán, Puebla
Right: PLATFORM
FROM THE TOP
OF THE POLE

48

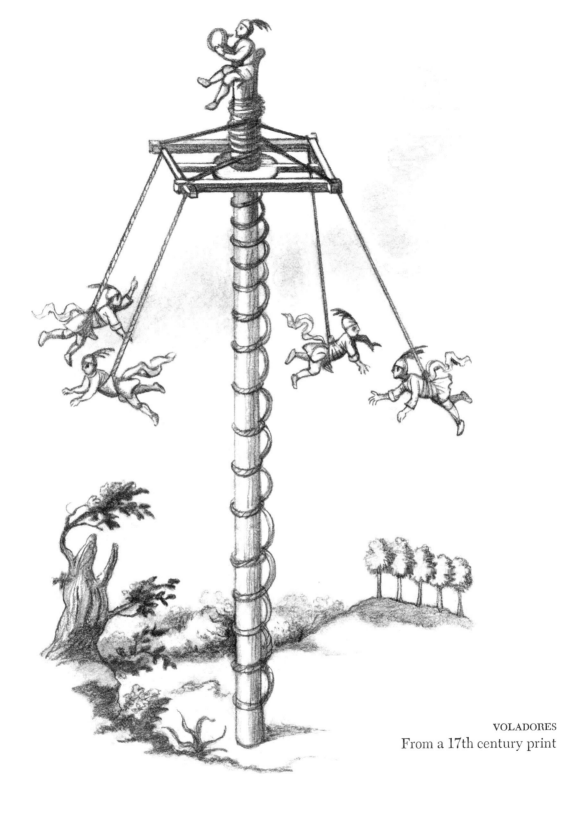

VOLADORES
From a 17th century print

TRADITIONAL
EUROPEAN
MAYTIME DANCE
From a painting by
Pieter Breughel, 1634

The dance of the Voladores originally symbolized the flight of four sacred birds of Indian mythology, linked to the four directions of the universe. In other sacred circle dances, the performers imitated the circular movement of the stars in the night sky, or paid homage to the great round sun.

While many of these dances have lost their old meanings, others are still solemn acts of worship in religious festivals. As the dancers revolve for many hours together, often to the endless rhythm of drums, they may go into a trance. They feel their bodies seized and controlled by the power of a god or a spirit. They become possessed.

50

In the land of Benin in West Africa, the people worship many gods through dancing. Every year, at a village festival in Benin, there is a circle dance in honor of a mighty god of earth, the giver of good crops, good fortune, and families of healthy children.

Early in the morning of the festival, the dancing place on the edge of the village is almost deserted, but under the tree in the center the musicians have started to play. Using drums, big and small, an iron gong, and a pair of basketwork rattles, they weave a complicated network of sound.

A few old women are dancing quietly on their own, with shuffling steps, from side to side. A man standing nearby is suddenly caught up in the insistent rhythm of the music. He flings himself into the air and dances with wild, twisting leaps, flourishing a bunch of green leaves in his hand.

More men and women drift onto the dancing
ground. They pass the shrine of the god, which stands
at one end like a large green bower, its entrance
screened by fresh-cut ferns. Some of the women have
shaven heads and white draperies, signs of their deep
devotion to the god.

Now the drum-rhythm quickens, and the people
begin running around the tree and the musicians. The
white-clad women are chanting as they run, and pointing skyward with graceful gestures of their hands.
The circle whirls faster, and sweat falls in great drops
from the brows of the dancers. On and on they run,
driven by the ceaseless rhythm of the drums, until

53

suddenly the circle bursts open. The dancers break free and race away up the road to the village in a long snaking line.

The music slows down. The space around the tree is empty except for the old women dancing gently from side to side. Small children wander about. A young boy joins the drummers and beats a big drum with unerring rhythm, while another, hardly more than a baby, proudly shakes a pair of heavy rattles.

Then there is shouting from the village. The dancers are returning! The musicians spring to life again and strike up a fast beat. The dancers come running at top speed bearing offerings for the god—great heavy bunches of green plantains and earthy roots of yam. They throw down their loads in front of the musicians, and then race around the tree in a dance of triumph and joy.

Women sway and bend, and men leap high, six abreast, spinning around with angular swings of their arms. Fresh dancers plunge into the whirling mass.

The white-clad women are chanting again, and someone screams, as though possessed by the spirit of the god. The dancing ground is flooded to the edges with a river of dancers, tossing and heaving to the rhythm of the drums.

At last the rhythm changes and slows to a jog-trotting pace. The spell is broken, and the magic circle falls apart. In a few moments, the dancers have scattered, and no one is left in the dusty space but a few children and the musicians under the tree.

The village will rest in the heat of the day, but later the dancing will begin again. Once more the dancers and musicians will make their act of homage to the god. Through the language of dance, they will pray for another year of good crops and good living in the mud-walled village under the palms.

Their prayer is the prayer of farming people the world over. Thousands of miles from the village in Benin is another village with houses the color of the earth, whose people also gather for day-long festivals of dance. The dancers move in a different pattern, to the rhythm of a different drum, but like the people of Benin, they speak through their dancing to the great forces of nature that control their world.

To these people, Pueblo Indians, the earth and the corn they plant in it are sacred. In the height of summer the sun has seared the land, the streams are dry, and the fields cry out for rain. So the Indians unite to bring the storm clouds and the rain through the power of dance.

bend to the earth

THE drum is beating in the pueblo of Santo Domingo. The long narrow plaza between the brown adobe houses is hot and dusty under the summer sun. The people clustered in the shade of the porches are waiting for the dancers to come. Their eyes are turned toward the great round brown wall of the sacred *kiva* that rises at one end of the plaza.

Suddenly a little group of figures comes leaping and dancing from behind the *kiva*. These are the *koshares*, the clowns and keepers of order. They wear black loincloths and rattles of horn and tortoiseshell. Faces, bodies and limbs are painted gray, and on their heads are close-fitting caps with topknots of dry cornhusks. Dancing freely and gracefully to the rhythm of the drum, the *koshares* circle and reach up with their hands to call down rain from the cloudless sky.

Now the standard-bearer appears, leaning backward under the weight of the long pole crowned with bright parrot feathers and the tall narrow banner with its design of a green cornplant. Behind him are the dancers. They come from the *kiva* in two endless lines—men in white kilts and women in short black gowns and upstanding wooden headdresses of turquoise blue.

The drummer, pounding on his great drum, marches beside them. The chorus of singers follows him, dressed in brilliant shirts and gaily striped trousers, with spruce twigs stuck in the backs of their silver-decorated belts. As the two lines of dancers turn inward to face each other, the singing begins, low and deep-throated. The song rises and falls like the sighing of wind in pine trees, and always beneath it is the beat of the drum, the pounding pulse that is the heart of the dance and song.

Now the dancers' lines are broken, and small groups cross past each other, circling, weaving in and out. The dancers move down the plaza toward the leafy green shrine of Santo Domingo, whose statue presides over the dance. The singers move down and back again beside the dancers. From the oldest singer to the tiniest dancing child, all are caught up in the tide of movement and sound, bound together in a common purpose. Every dancer and singer is there to speak to the earth, to call to the earth to bring forth fruit and the sky to send down rain.

All the morning until midday the dancing goes on in the sun-scorched plaza, alternating between the

two groups of dancers from the two *kivas* of the pueblo. The second group comes out with a fresh standard-bearer, drummer, and singers, and with new *koshares*, painted in black stripes or designs of raindrops or open hands. These *koshares*, like the first ones, are quick to do their duty as keepers of order, mending a dancer's disheveled costume or pushing back spectators who come too close.

After the midday rest, there is drumming again in the plaza. A bigger crowd has gathered there, under the porches and on the flat roofs of the earth-brown houses. When the dancers and singers come again, the pace is faster. Each dance begins with strange, high-pitched cries from the *koshares*. On the heavy beats of the drum, the dancers dip their heads and bend down toward the earth, with sweeping gestures of the green spruce twigs in their hands.

Old men break from the chorus and join the dancers. One of them, almost too feeble to lift his feet, dances on and on by himself, while the rest of the chorus surges past him like an army. Their singing has become an earth-sound, no longer the music of human throats; and the drumbeat is the pulse of life itself.

The power of the dance is almost too much for the watchers to bear. They are part of the worship and the prayer, the bending to the earth, the cry to the rainless sky. The drumbeat has become the rhythm of their own bodies, felt deep within, and every change in the beat is a jarring pain.

The wind rises and whips up a stinging storm of dust. The lines of dancers, black, white, and green, and the brilliant colors of the singers, all merge together in a golden haze.

Then a great shadow sweeps over the plaza. Clouds have piled up in the sky and smothered the sun. And still the dance goes on through the whirling dust and the deepening gloom.

At last the rain comes, big drops flung by the wind, dark spots of water on the dusty earth, coolness on the faces of the people. The wind blows cold, and colder still is the rain—rain and more rain for the growing corn and the thirsty ground, the promise of new life for the earth and its people.

Through the magic of dance, the people have spoken their prayer, united as one with the rhythms of earth and sky. They have danced as their ancestors did, when the world was young; and now, as the dancing ends with the close of day, the prayer is answered.

Hunza

India

Burma
Thailand
Cambodia

Philippines

Pacific Ocean

MICRONESIA

Ulithi

Yap

Ponape

Papua New Guinea

Solomon Is.

POLYNESIA

Sarawak

Bali

Fiji

Samoa

Cook Islands

Australia

New
Zealand

PUEBLO
INDIANS

Atlantic
Ocean

Mexico

Sierra Leone
Ivory Coast
Benin

POKOT
PEOPLE

DANCE
MAP

CHRISTINE PRICE'S distinguished books are unique. In both text and illustration she has succeeded admirably in evoking the quality of life and culture in many remote parts of the world. Her dominant theme has been the importance of art and things of the spirit in the lives of the people whom she has come to know and love.

Her books include *The Mystery of Masks, Dancing Masks of Africa, Talking Drums of Africa, Arts of Wood,* and *Arts of Clay.*